A Sacred Place For Learning:
Teaching, Leading & Culture

Written By Naim Q. Sanders

Copyright © 2020 by Naim Q. Sanders for Naim Sanders LLC

All rights reserved.

ISBN: 9798642057667
ISBN: 13- 9798642057667

DEDICATIONS

To God for the gift of writing and experiences to write about.

To my mother who instilled in me the value of education.

To all the teachers, school leaders and staff members who serve students and families.

TABLE OF CONTENTS

Foreword	7
Preface	10
Introduction	16

SACRED TEACHING

Soul of Teaching	23
The Divine & Splendid	28
Allure of Being Busy	33
The Right Swing	36
Limitations	43
Never Lose Your Humanity	47
Stay Focused	50
Being Nice	52
It's About Will Power	56

SACRED LEADING

Late Night Rhythm	61
Mental Toughness	66
There Will Be Conflict	74
Stay Calm	82
Know the Landscape	87
Love and Gratitude	91
None of Your Business	94
Embrace Your Experiences	98
Protect Your Ears	102

TABLE OF CONTENTS

SACRED CULTURE

Adapting to Change	106
Fresh Starts	110
Don't Throw Stones	113
The Kind of Schools You Want	116
Identity Crisis	118
The Trend of Trauma	124
Conclusion	128
Notes	130
About the Author	143
Contact Information	144

Foreword

A Sacred Place for Learning: *Teaching, Leading and Culture*

Leadership is not about putting out fires or placing bandages on problems. It is not about making people happy, winning their approval or getting the masses to "buy in" as if competing in some illustrious popularity contest. Leadership is about serving people and thinking beyond today, this year or even next year. It is about looking into the future and systematically building relationships and multi-faceted networks among very unique and complex individuals in order to create an ecosystem that will fortify, strengthen and refine the culture for years to come. Leadership is all about intentionally cultivating and tending a living and breathing environment that becomes . . . A Sacred Place for Learning.

In order to be classified as a living organism, an organism must change and grow. Vijayendra Mohanty once stated that, "to hold something sacred means valuing something enough to let it change you."

I can honestly state from my own personal and corporate encounters with Mr. Naim Sanders, that he has made our school holy ground by treating each and every part of our school community as if we have been consecrated or set apart and empowered for the work we have been called to do. We are different. We are transforming. We have changed and we continue to change some more. His innate ability to see through the veneer of what we may think we should present to the world falls away in his presence. When we are confused, he brings clarity. When we fall short, he nonjudgmentally inspires and guides us to be our best selves, adults and children alike.

As I have stated in times past, he has restored dignity to the profession of teaching. Truly, Mr. Sanders has been endowed with an uncommon enablement to breathe life into burned-out teachers, bring hope to overwhelmed parents and acceptance to students who may have otherwise slipped through the cracks in our educational system.

A Sacred Place for Learning: *Teaching, Leading and Culture* is the type of book that will connect you with your authentic self. It will encourage you to remain grounded while kindling hope for the future during ever increasing times of change. It will remind you that you are not in control and that is okay. Through the window of Mr. Sander's life experiences as an educator and leader, you will encounter a window to your soul. Enjoy the journey through the hallowed pages of a book that was written with you in mind.

Mrs. Lisa L. Hayes

TESOL Specialist

A Sacred Place For Learning: *Teaching, Leading & Culture*

Preface

In March of 2020, just a few months before this book was published, the Coronavirus had a devastating impact on schools, education, students and teachers in the state of Ohio when our Governor, Mike DeWine, ordered all schools in the state to stop having students attend school for an "extended spring break"(4 weeks total). During this time, students would be provided with learning opportunities that would come in the form of on-line learning. This was an unprecedented order and schools, not only in Ohio but across the country, have been impacted by it. As of now, the effect will last four weeks but there is already chatter that it may last longer and potentially lead to students not attending school for the remainder of the year. (School buildings eventually closed to students and teachers taught online for the remainder of the year). What we know as students physically attending schools has been replaced by learning in their home environment with instruction being led or facilitated by parents, guardians and teachers on line.

It does not take much to imagine the panic and worry that this has created among many educators, parents, district leaders and the community as a whole. As a principal of an elementary school with a little over 600 students, 95% free and reduced lunch and a high English learner population, there were a lot of questions, concerns and unknown factors. My first priority before allowing negative thoughts and worry to overly consume me, was to listen and seek guidance from district leaders.

On one Thursday afternoon, all principals in my district were called to an emergency administrators' meeting to hear the latest orders from the Governor in regards to schools being closed for four weeks (one week included spring break) and the steps we would take as a district in response of the order. Without going into a ton of details and technical information, principals were given the charge to meet with their building staff the following day and implement a plan to send home with students all of their personal items, school supplies, books and potentially a Chromebook (one per household) for online learning that our teachers would provide. That night before my meeting with my staff, I had a million things going through my head and it was a long night of processing. I wanted to reduce the stress and anxiety that my staff may have been experiencing by communicating the facts and dispelling any false information or propaganda (There was enough of that going around already). My intentions were to present myself in a calm manner so that teachers and staff members would feel confident when serving students that day and remain calm as well. I truly believe that the attitude, behaviors and disposition of a leader spreads to those they are leading. My last goal on this day was to mobilize my team to do specific tasks in order to prepare students to be absent from school for four weeks in the midst of a pandemic crisis. I had four important meetings by 9:30 a.m. to get the day started as best as possible. The first meeting was with my teaching staff, secondly with non-teaching staff, then I met with a selective team of individuals who I trusted to carry our specific duties and then finally convened with my instructional coaches in order to ensure that all bases were covered. In all it was a good day considering the circumstances. The ultimate goal was to remain calm in the midst of uncertain times and a potentially chaotic situation. I wanted desperately for teachers and staff to know that even though we did know how this was going to end we could be assured that we would get through it together. I wanted to set the tone for how people would respond to these unfamiliar circumstances and I wanted my attitude, behavior and responses to make a difference in how other people responded.

I wrote about 99% of this book before the Coronavirus impacted our schools and the manuscript has been waiting to go to the editor which I consider a blessing because it has allowed me to rewrite the preface based on these current times. I truly believe that schools are a sacred place but even more so now in our present days. The spread of the Coronavirus has left me with a heavy heart for the families that are stressed about how they are going to feed their children, those who are worried about childcare and ultimately families that are under the pressure of having to manage the situation. This experience is showing me how sacred a place schools are, not only for learning, but also for the emotional and social growth of students. The love, compassion, support and relationships that children form with teachers can never be duplicated through E-learning but this is the hand that has been dealt so we have to play the cards.

For as long as I am able to, I want to maintain the sacredness of schools, the hopefulness of educators and the culture of prosperity for students who occupy the classrooms. I think that as a society we need to reestablish the sacredness of schools, what education provides for humanity and the work of professionals who labor tirelessly to serve students, families and society. This book is for everyone who works relentlessly to provide a sacred place for young people from custodians to secretaries, instructional aides, teachers, support specialists and school leaders. Your work is often thankless, challenges appear impossible, but someway and somehow you successfully find ways to get things done. I hope that *A Sacred Place For Learning: Teaching, Leading & Culture* will serve as a reminder for all of the great work that you do, reaffirm your beliefs in the positive difference that schools make in society and provide support and new knowledge for you to learn in the process.

Introduction

A Sacred Place

"If you have a sacred place and use it, take advantage of it, something will happen."
-Joseph Campbell

From an early age, I was always taught that school was a sacred place. My mom is a woman that viewed education as very important and crucial, almost to the point of it being a matter of life and death. As I have grown and matured as a man, I have come to share her value of education. Currently I am an elementary school principal and I have served on almost every level of education a person can serve. If you add my total years of life at age 43, from birth to now, I have spent roughly 38 years in school as a student in K-12 education, an undergraduate student, graduate student, teacher, adjunct professor, charter school developer, assistant principal, principal and consultant with the state department of education. I have seen and experienced many of the highs and lows of being in school and it has served as a sacred place for me both personally and professionally for the majority of my life. If you are a professional who works in schools and have done so for some time then it might be that you too have spent the majority of your life being in school as well. I have watched the lives of adults and children be positively and negatively impacted by their encounters and the events at school for decades. Adults remember the influence of teachers throughout their lives and share stories about their school experiences with their own children for generations. Teachers are remembered for the words they use when motivating their students and unfortunately any disparaging comments that may damage a student's soul as well. Almost everyone remembers the school culture that has helped shaped who they are well into adulthood. No other institution with professionals can have a lasting impact on the minds of people like schools do, and for that reason we must always remember the sacredness of teaching, leading and culture.

In my opinion, schools are like no other institutions on the planet in the sense that people with different life experiences, values, beliefs, ethnicities, races, religions, disabilities as well as other differences and similarities come together in one place for a common goal of learning and being educated at ages ranging from early childhood to old age. Schools are a sacred place where students and educators unite for the purpose of enriching their lives, investing time and resources to improve their quality of living or to improve the lives of others and create better opportunities. Schools are forced to meet the ongoing demands of society because schools themselves are a society for people to come into contact with their future, learn about their past, find out their flaws, learn about their brilliance and everything in between. Schools are sacred because they create order for humanity, they are intended to bridge gaps between poverty and prosperity and they introduce people from all walks of life that may not have had the opportunity to engage in learning about different cultures, ethnicities, experiences and otherwise. Schools are sacred because of what they provide that many other institutions are unable to do. Schools provide children and youth with an education, experiences to prepare them for the real world, they tend to the needs of students and their families, they provide a safe environment away from their parents and in some instances better than their families. Needs are met individually and collectively. Deep consideration on how to serve the needs of young people in regards to their mental health and well-being is woven into the fabric of education regardless of race, gender, disabilities or religion. Without the sacred place of schools, we would be absent of so much in the world and miss out on the beautiful struggles of life and education. Without schools, society would miss having a place where students can gather in one place to have their needs met, their issues addressed and be given an opportunity to move from dependent to independent thinking and prosperity in life.

My intent of writing this book is simply to share my stories, thoughts and experiences in hopes that they can help anyone reading these pages. I want to inspire you to keep trying and never give up, motivate you to be your very best and educate you in ways about teaching, leading, learning and culture that you may have not thought of before. If you are an educator then the first thing that you have to understand is that there is no way of getting around the beautiful struggles that education provides.

When reading this book, do not feel that you have to read it from the first page to the last page in chronological order (I would never know if you did anyway). Look at the Table of Contents, and pick a topic that interests you the most or find something that you may be dealing with in your own experiences as an educator. You have my permission to skip around, read a bit, stop, reflect and then read some more. Perhaps it takes you a few days, weeks or even months to complete the book and that is okay. It is simply about you getting what you need and what you want as an educator.

SACRED TEACHING

1

Soul of Teaching

"Your greatest legacy isn't your dream; it's the dream you inspire in others. You aren't just a dreamer; you are a dreamcatcher" -Mark Batterson

The basic definition of the word soul is, "the spiritual or immaterial part of a human being regarded as immortal." Another definition of soul is, "an emotional or intellectual energy or intensity, especially as revealed in a work of art or an artistic performance." In my own words I would describe soul as an unseen force that connects human beings with other human beings in order to provide them with the essentials in life. Souls are the greatest connector known to humanity and our universe. You may be able to connect students to grade level content to ensure their preparation for the next grade level. You may even be successful in helping a child to mature and prepare for working collaboratively with their peers. However, when you connect with a child's soul, you are providing them with the substance they need to fulfill their destiny in life and that alone makes all of the difference in the world.

Without our souls, we are meaningless, we have no purpose and we ultimately fall short of living a fulfilling life. There have been thousands of books written about schools, education, teaching, students, school culture, leadership and learning. Education is, without question, one of the most important systems, processes or complex structures in our human society. It is so important that the U.S. government spent around nine billion dollars in education in 2018 (including higher education). That spending alone demonstrates the investment that tax payers make on something that is so important to us all. Many well-written authors and scholars have penned books on the subject of education. These books are descriptive on what to do, philosophical in regards to what is meaningful and impactful in the lives of teachers, students, administrators, parents and other stakeholders.

Few, to my knowledge, (for whatever that is worth) involve the soul of teaching. In essence, the soul of teaching establishes a connection to students that stretches beyond the touchable curriculum, standards and even everyday interactions. It is our link to the souls of students that propels them to their greater purpose when we choose to allow ourselves to serve as vessels in this sacred process. It stretches far beyond what we can sense. It is our faith in what we know that allows us to serve students in this manner. Which leads me to ask why there is little acknowledgement or awareness on the impact of teaching from the soul. If teaching and education is so important to millions of people, impacts so many lives, employs so many professionals and can serve as a gateway to prosperity, then why do we neglect to mention the soul of teaching and choose to keep a surface level focus that includes only standards, curriculum, pedagogy and assessments. In my opinion, things that are as important as the soul and teaching are too vital to the lives of generations to take such a shallow approach as to only discuss what is on a surface level. More importantly, teaching and learning deserve a much deeper examination of their impact on the lives of students and we need to give deeper thought to the impact of teaching on the souls of students and teachers. In fact, I believe with all of the curricula, instructional strategies, brain development research, behavior management systems, innovations in technology, professional development and the list goes on, we neglect the one deep thing beneath the human skin that is so important to life which is, the human soul. You never know how what you say to a child in the third grade impacts their soul. It can, plant a seed and motivate them to do great things as an adult. You might be unaware that the hug you give a student may serve as the one reassurance in life that everything will be okay in the end. You may not be cognizant of the fact that the love you give is the only love that your student receives and that love is enough to carry them through the toughest times that they encounter. We all have a soul and the soul impacts our character, decisions, thoughts and beliefs. It essentially determines what we do and do not do in life.

Without the soul we are nothing and without teaching from the soul it is very unlikely that quality learning can even occur. I believe that there is a sacred connection between the soul, teaching and learning. I also believe that this concept deserves extensive discussion. You can learn the best pedagogy that there is, your students can be great learners who soak up all of the information you teach and you can even have exemplary classroom management, resulting in exceptional student compliance. However, if you ignore the soul in your teaching and learning then you will miss more than you could have gained in touching the lives of students.

2

The Divine & Splendid

"Nothing splendid has ever been achieved except by those who dared believe that something inside of them was superior to circumstances."
-Bruce Barton

In the dark, both the divine and splendid can feel like they are righteous and both can be unjust. Teaching is not always about being divine or splendid. Teaching requires having a deeper consciousness about the needs of others, especially students. Way too often those who are responsible for the lives of children or youth ignore conscious thinking because they are bombarded with outside forces that dictate how they should think and how they should perform. These outside forces can be well intended but it does not always make them right. It is not uncommon for both the divine and the splendid to have good intentions but to be equally improper in there pursuits to educate students.

Imagine for a moment that the divine and splendid are joined together with a similar goal to do what is best, but they have different beliefs. The divine believe that putting children first is about attending to their emotional and social needs while not completely meeting students' academic needs. The divine want to ensure students are happy, feel good about themselves and have a high self-esteem regardless of what they accomplish. In essence, from the perspective of the divine, there are no losers in life and everyone is a winner, everyone gets a trophy and showing up and trying is enough. This may not be wrong in the minds of the divine but it is a one-sided viewpoint because sacrificing quality instruction and learning for students' feelings without mastering content is a potentially dangerous sacrifice. In the end, the divine have students who feel good about themselves but lack academic achievement and growth. They value children but potentially lack an awareness of the academic components of learning.

Then you have the side of the splendid. The splendid want students to learn at any and every cost, even if that means ignoring the social and emotional needs of students. For the splendid, it is not about feelings or well-being, it is about working, working hard and blocking out any distractions that prevent a student from focusing on academics even if the distractions are legitimate. The splendid teacher adheres to the cerebral approach which involves assessments, student achievement data and learning the curriculum. The splendid could care less about teaching to the core essence of who a student is on the inside and what enhances the inner being of students. They are motivated and impressed with their own abilities to help students improve academically and raise scores on their tests while being much less concerned about a students' character growth and development.

Conflict arises because both divine and splendid teachers fail to see where either side is coming from. Ultimately, they choose one mindset over the other because they are unable to strike a balance between the two. Being divine *and* splendid stretches them too much.

Sacred teachers need to have an overabundance of both perspectives in order to meet their obligation to teaching and learning. The needs of children are great and to ignore one side while clinging to the other results in an unbalanced, one-sided approach that shortchanges learners. The ways of the divine teacher and the ways of the splendid teacher will always be intertwined to fully educate, motivate and inspire each individual student. Do not sacrifice one for the other nor fall victim to undermining one while neglecting the other. Children come to us with gaps that need to be filled, needs that have to be met and many imperfections that need to be refined. For instance, you may have a child that has grown up in a very transient household and is always moving from place to place. At school this child may be possessive of their things because they feel their things are all that they have. They may find security in their desk, school supplies and the items they receive in school. This student may fight for his/her place in line; however, it is not about being in line, it is about having a secured place.

To be a divine teacher without being a splendid teacher is an injustice to students. Likewise, being a splendid teacher without being divine is equally neglectful and unjust. Students need a balance of both splendid and divine teaching without compromising one for the other This ensures that the whole child is educated and acquires the lessons needed to become healthy and productive human beings.

3

Allure of Being Busy

"Being busy and being productive are two different things." -Unknown

In order to accomplish more, it means that you have to be able to relinquish control of things that you honestly have little to no control over. We live in a world where it is popular to be busy and attractive to "look" important. We tend to be busy answering emails, talking on the phone, spending hours positing things on social media and going places that we really do not want to go in order to, accomplish nothing other than to, say we went. Being busy has become a popular trend to signify that the busier you are the more productive you are. Busyness without productivity has somehow woven itself into the thinking of educators. They are slowly killing themselves mentally and physically to be productive with the best of intentions but with little results. Being busy has become such a dominant mindset that educators have failed to be strategic in their actions as well as their work. Sacred educators know that being busy is overrated. They prefer to be productive with their time because they know that a busy person is not always a productive person. Productivity requires having a focus on what you want to accomplish, a realization of what needs be done along with an understanding of what does not require much attention since many things organically take care of themselves. Do not be a busy, unproductive educator who does everything except for what is most important. Refrain from being drawn into the allure of being busy because it is popular among colleagues and the profession of teaching. In my experience, sacred teachers move gracefully throughout the classroom like an elegant ballerina or skilled gymnast with coordinated movements and calculated steps that do not waste energy. They are smooth, intentional and polished. Every action and step is flawless, maximizing opportunities for students to learn. They are purposeful and strategic but most importantly they are able to successfully distinguish between what is necessary and what is not necessary in helping their students obtain and maximize high student achievement.

4

The Right Swing

"Life was throwing curve balls at me left and right, but then God gave me a bat and showed me how to swing." -Unknown

Teachers have a lot of challenges coming at them on a daily basis. I am of the belief that teachers need to know how to react and respond to these challenges correctly. Sacred teachers learn to absorb the necessary skills and knowledge specific to serving *their* student populations while refraining from relying on general knowledge and skills that may not always meet the needs of the students they are teaching. When teachers do not possess the suitable skills and knowledge required for meeting the needs of their specific group of students, they can expect to encounter many curveballs simply because they are unprepared. It is not uncommon for teachers to have different experiences, different values and different belief systems about learning and education than students and students' families.

In order to be an effective educator, it is important to pursue diverse experiences in an effort to connect learning with the needs of students. Openness to change is advantageous but perhaps more vitally importantly, is a teacher's ability to reshape any personal biases or previous training that does not meet the current demands of their pupils. It is not just about the knowledge, skills and experiences that educators have but it is more about having the "right" knowledge, skills and experiences in order to best serve students.

Imagine for a moment that you are learning to hit a small ball. In order to be effective at hitting the small ball, you need to spend adequate time practicing and preparing your swing. To do this and become successful at it, you take all of the necessary steps. These steps may include reading about hitting a small ball, watching YouTube videos, researching and receiving advice from others on techniques and so on. After some studying and research, you start the physical work by practicing the right stance, ensuring that your arms are in the right position, focusing your eyes on the ball and even taking some practice swings. Over time you begin to get comfortable, and you even experience some success in hitting that small ball. Now that you feel good about your research, observations and practice, you feel comfortable about your swing in hitting the small ball and you are ready for the test to see how successful your preparation has been. You get in position as you have practiced and focus on your task of hitting the small ball. However, there is a snag. I inform you that the small ball that you will be hitting is not like the small ball you have been practicing your swing on. Instead of assessing how well you hit a golf ball (small ball) I assess you by how you hit a baseball (small ball). The small ball you have been practicing hitting is immobile, sits on a tee and is hit best by swinging downward. The baseball I assess you with hitting is thrown at you and can be hit by swinging in a variety of directions depending on how the ball is thrown. Since you assumed it was a golf ball (small ball) that you would be hitting, that is how you focused your research and practice. Other than the goal of hitting a "small ball", your training has now become irrelevant in preparation for the task and assessment. The ball you will be assessed with will be thrown at you in the form of a pitch instead of sitting on a golf tee for which you have been preparing. You are smart enough to realize, that the problem is not necessarily your swing and it is not the ball. The problem is essentially your preparation. You have been preparing to hit a ball that requires a much different swing than the one you will be assessed on hitting. You can make the argument that both balls are small and you need a long object (golf club or bat) to hit them successfully. However, the swings are not the same and there lies the gap in achieving your goal.

Being prepared to serve students can be very similar. In education, we know and understand that student improvement is important, we know that it will require hard work, we also understand that it takes practice, focus and even learning from others. However, we do not always consider our environment, school culture, nor the specific needs of students as we prepare. In fact, we are not intentional about identifying the specific needs students have in order to educate them appropriately and this can result in failure if we do not prepare properly. You will not necessarily fail because you are incapable, the failure is the result of the wrong swing because you have spent time preparing incorrectly, like aiming at the wrong small ball.

Teachers go to college to get the preparation they need, they pass state exams that are requirements for certification, they read about issues pertaining to education, study curricula and best practices for teaching but neglect to reflect on whether or not what they are doing is right for their particular students and environment. Many well-intentioned and good-hearted teachers try their very best and become exhausted, deflated and receive unfair criticism not because they are incompetent, but because they have been prepared improperly. Sometimes your preparation in teaching whether through your college training or professional development can lead you to believe that all students are the same, they all have the same needs and they all come from the same environments. As a result, many teachers have the wrong swings because they have been trained by similar methods.

The point is this: students, schools, cultures, student needs, districts and communities are all different. Sure there are many similarities, like "small balls" but many more differences exist and these differences are what propose unique challenges in teaching, leading and culture. You may need overlapping and common skills that are included in good teaching practices. However, the skills needed in every environment are not the same and that is where many teachers, principals and administrators fail to see the difference. Within every group there are exceptions and sub-groups.

Do not fall victim to thinking that all groups, are the same, all students are the same, all communities are the same, all schools are the same and all needs are the same because that is far from the truth. As a sacred teacher, practice and prepare your swing and be sure that you have the right swing for your target in addition to what your students will need.

5

Limitations

"We all have limitations in our lives. It is when we accept these limitations that we can see beyond them and excel." -Unknown

You will have limitations in teaching and leading students. That is natural because we are all limited in one way or another. We are humans that can sometimes do superhuman things and this is in no way intended to downplay the power and abilities we have, it is just a reality of life. Everyone has a "particular set of skills" as Liam Neeson would say (watch the movie, *Taken*) and whatever your particular set of skills may be, it does not mean that you are able to do everything for every child at every moment. Instead of getting frustrated and giving up because of the things that you are not able to do, you have other options to consider. Those options include getting the help you need from others in order to do better for your students and taking time to reflect on what you are doing.

We will not fail students if we choose to not give up and if we seek resources that serve our pursuits in educating students. Getting help for students can come in a multitude of forms. The help can be from people such as colleagues, parents, administrators, counselors, specialists or friends outside of work who might be connected to your situation. Everyone has a particular set of skills and some skills that other educators possess you may not have yourself. Do not be ashamed if you do not have the same skills as other educators. You are unique and your uniqueness is an asset to you and can be critical for making a positive difference in the lives of your students. Although you have limitations, be open to growing and improving. The good news is, your limitations may not be the limitations of someone else and you can get the support that you need when you need it.

Seeking Help

I like to use staff meetings to allow teachers to share best practices. During this time, teachers provide information in regards to what is going well in their classrooms and they give examples of whatever they may be struggling with at the time. This gives other teachers an opportunity to learn from their colleagues, identify their own strengths and analyze areas in need of improvement. In my opinion, this is a better use of time than having teachers listen to a lot of gibberish from me (although I think my gibberish is entertaining). I have found that it is easier for some people to get help during a staff meeting, especially those teachers who feel that they need to have it all figured out. Teachers are unfairly expected to know everything and that is simply unrealistic. Educators need a platform of resources and materials from colleagues where they can learn, grow and help one another overcome their weaknesses in a way that makes them feel good and not guilty. The misbelief that teachers should have all of the answers is irrational and results in unnecessarily high anxiety.

Be A Constant Learner

As an educator, you should never stop feeding your mind. There are a multitude of opportunities for you to learn and decrease your limitations as an adult educator. Never lose your love for learning nor stop seeking opportunities to grow from other people (good examples and bad examples). Learn from your own failures by reflecting on what you did successfully and unsuccessfully. Do your research on your craft by studying issues that pertain to teaching, leading, culture and learning. Read and remain a student of learning. Be open to new ideas and concepts. Sacred teachers are always open to discovering new things while resisting the temptation to believe that they know all that there is to know. I encourage you to be a sponge that is constantly absorbing fresh knowledge, ideas, practices and information.

6

Never Lose Your Humanity

"Be soft. Do not let the world make you hard. Do not let pain make you hate. Do not let bitterness steal your sweetness. Take pride that even though the rest of the world may disagree, you still believe it to be a beautiful place."
-Kurt Vonnegut

Humanity is what brings us all together. Regardless of race, culture, age, gender, experiences and beliefs we all share one thing in common; we are all human. As human beings we all have basic needs that are widespread and needs that are not so basic but are often shared amongst each of us. At times education tends to separate us and makes us forget the humanity that we all share. We are naturally separated in schools by locations, grade levels, abilities, available resources, performances and so much more but still the commonality that we all share is our humanity. Sacred teachers never lose their humanity in what they are doing for students and what they do for their colleagues.

Losing your humanity will cause you to lose sight of your purpose in teaching and leading. Never make the mistake of putting "things" before people. Sacred teachers understand that they are not meant to serve things, therefore, they serve people. Based upon our conversations and actions, I often think that we forget we are serving people. We talk about standards, curricula, assessments, books, subject content, schedules and so much more but we lose sight of the fact that none of these things are as important as the life of a human being, both children and adults. When the conversations center more around things and less about humans we lose our humanity and when this is done, we fail students and one another regardless of what the test scores may be.

I believe that great schools meet the needs of the students, adults and families in the school through service. The needs vary from school to school and from community to community and it creates challenges that are not always easy to define, let alone meet. However, working together to meet the needs of humanity will eventually take care of the things that we sometimes overvalue in education. The stress, pressure and anxiety that educators frequently feel results in distraction. When distractions occur, the needs of humanity are not met and people suffer at the expense of things that tend to have little value in the overall worth of education. Sacred teachers, never forget their responsibility is to human beings and not things. They consider what is important for humans and not what things are more important than humans. No matter how difficult the job becomes, no matter how great the responsibility is, never under any circumstance forget that you are where you are to serve humanity. So never lose that mindset.

7

Stay Focused

"You have to focus if you want to learn. Keeping your mind on track is essential."
-Tony Payne

Staying focused can be difficult especially when you consider all of the distractions that teachers have coming at them daily. Focusing in the moment is essential and there are times when you need to step back from a situation to analyze it more thoroughly, refocus yourself and fully process the situation. Staying focused allows you to look more intensely at the situation but you must also have the maturity to look at it from all sides. Staying focused involves taking the attention off of yourself and looking at things from the viewpoint of those around you including your students. We are born with an innate ability to focus solely on our own needs regardless of how those needs impact others (Think of a newborn baby). Staying focused is about removing the distractions that prevent us from being at our best. Sacred teachers understand that they must keep their focus on their students rather than themselves in order to meet the needs of students no matter how difficult this may be. It is almost impossible to be positively influential in the lives of students if we obsess over our own needs. If you see your needs as greater than the needs of others, this will prevent you from doing what is in the best interest of those whom you are intended to serve. This creates additional limitations that become counterproductive to the difference that you seek to make. Remember to stay focused on what your students need, understand your own abilities in molding their minds and strive to be a positive role model for your students with the aim of helping them reach their full potential.

8

Being Nice

"I want you to be nice...until it's time to not be nice."
-Patrick Swayze

This may come across a little harsh, especially for my colleagues in education but being nice will not always get you the results that you want. There is a time to be nice and a time where being nice simply does not work! Allow me to elaborate by saying that this does not mean you should be rude, disrespectful, hurtful, unsympathetic, negative or cynical toward your students or your colleagues. Nor am I implying that you should throw empathy out the window or become uncaring towards the feelings of others. The point that I want to make is that sometimes being nice may send the message that you are not serious about what you want, what you need and what you expect from students because you are not always direct when you are nice. Unfortunately, the culture that has been established for teachers does not take them seriously nor does it expect them to advocate for themselves as they should. I believe that teachers need to be viewed as professionals who have valuable contributions to add to their craft and to the lives of their students. Teachers essentially deal with demands and challenges that not many other professionals face and they are still expected to just be nice, come what may. Being nice is a good thing but it is not always the most appropriate thing, especially when you have tried being nice and it has not produced the results that you want.

I have spent many years as an elementary school principal and that means that I have worked closely with kindergarten students as well. Let me tell you, kindergarten students are the cutest, whether they are my own biological children or my students at school. They can be very active, curious, rambunctious and have a zeal for life that most adults can learn from. Kindergarten teachers are incredible as well. They are typically loving, patient, kind and they have the coolest "teacher voices" when talking to students and occasionally when talking to adults when they are "out of character" as teachers. However, I have heard some of the best kindergarten teachers lose their smile, deepen their tones and shorten their sentences with kindergarten students because they were either being unsafe, hurt their peers or their behavior needed to be corrected for the sake of learning. This does not mean that the kindergarten teacher loved the students any less or lost their ability to be nice. It just means that being nice was not the best approach for the situation in order to effectively get done what needed to be done or to stop what inevitably needed to be stopped. In reality being nice will not always do the trick. Just like a carpenter needs more than a single hammer to build a house, a sacred teacher will always need a variety of tools in their toolbox and multiple approaches to serve their students. It is important to know what to do and have a variety of skills to be able to do it.

There is never any good reason to demean, disrespect, dehumanize or crush students' spirits. You have permission to be direct, to be stern and to demand the very best out of your students and that may not always come across as being nice! It means that you need to be serious about what you are saying and students need to understand that you are serious about learning, their safety and their overall well-being.

9

It's About Will Power

"Will power is the key to success. Successful people strive no matter what they feel by applying their will to overcome apathy, doubt or fear."
-Dan Millman

I have worked with hundreds of teachers in my career. A few were ineffective, but most fell somewhere in between skilled and highly effective. Regardless, there is one thing above all other things that separated an ineffective teacher from a highly effective teacher. That one thing is "will power". Will power can be described as the ability to control oneself. It also means having a strong determination that allows a person to do something difficult. It sounds rather easy and simple but actually I think it is a lot more challenging than it appears. The complexity of will power is that it is not always noticeable initially but neither is a lack of will power. On the surface all teachers can appear similar. It is not until a teacher is faced with some sort of adversity that the separation between ineffective, skilled and highly effective becomes glaringly visible. Will power is what separates teachers who are successful in overcoming some of the most problematic challenges they face from those who give up either physically or mentally. Teachers with strong will power do not just talk the talk, they walk the walk and do it by going the extra mile. This does not mean that they always have a good day, or that things always go their way or that they have the least challenging students. It only means they use their will power to respond to things appropriately and possess a mindset of not giving up. They work smarter than their peers which allows them to accomplish more and they have the unique ability to see and understand what is important in teaching while maximizing effort and time. Ultimately, they use their will power to do what is best for students and they believe that no matter how great the struggle may be, they are determined to be successful in getting the job done and done effectively. Will power allows sacred teachers to successfully adapt to uncomfortable situations and circumstances while courageously facing any and all challenges. When your will power is solid, you will always be able to stand and be strong in the midst of any turmoil. Consider will power like a strong oak tree with deep roots. Just like an oak tree you may experience the conditions of a harsh storm, however, like an oak tree, after the storm has passed you are still standing strong. It does not necessarily mean that the oak tree has not struggled to stand tough or has not taken its abuse over time, it just means that there is a refusal to fall, a refusal to be knocked down and a deeper refusal to lose its foundation. It is the will power that keeps it standing and remain standing.

Your will power allows you to do great things for your students and in teaching. The subject you teach, the standards you use, the lesson plans you write and the activities you provide for students are not equal to the will power that you possess. The good news for you is that will power can be developed, it can grow stronger and everyone has it regardless of race, ethnicity, gender, or experiences. Will power is simply a choice that you make. So grasp it. No one can keep it from you. Will power creates more opportunities for growth even in some of the most challenging experiences.

SACRED LEADING

10

Late Night Rhythm

"Control your own destiny or someone else will." -Jack Welsh

I am a night owl and have been so for over 20 years as a result of the birth of my oldest son, Zuriel who was born while I was in my final year of college. Zuriel was not much of a sleeper as a newborn so I had the responsibility of feeding, changing diapers and entertaining him at night while his mother, a college student as well, got some sleep. This also created a rhythm for me to get work done since I was awake at night with my son. Zuriel and I had a lot of late nights together until he eventually got into a sleeping pattern and abandoned me. So, here I am over 20 years later still staying up late at night working, thinking and creating. Honestly for me, staying up late at night is some sort of addiction. I love the stillness, the silence and the reflection time that the night brings. In fact, when my two youngest sons, Ethan and

Liam, are running around the house it is nearly impossible for me to concentrate on work so I spend my time with my family instead and choose to refrain from working. I cannot tell you how many times I have laid down in bed before 10 p.m. only to toss and turn for hours before being able to fall asleep. I have embraced my rhythm of late nights. Sure there are times, on the weekends especially, that I catch up on some sleep with afternoon naps or press reset on the alarm clock in the morning. But I still have my rhythm and my rhythm allows me to accomplish more things than most people who go to bed early. My late night rhythm provides me with the time to develop my dreams, my goals, reflect on my day, think about how to serve others and develop my thoughts. I had no clue 20 years ago that the work that I would do today would be accomplished because of the training I received from a newborn baby who could not sleep at night. I was developing a pattern for how I would conduct my professional work life in the years to come. As a teacher, I worked with students during the day, went home to spend time with my family and reserved late nights for grading papers, looking at student data, earning a master's degree and preparing for the next day. Much has not changed since becoming a principal. As a school leader, I use the day to meet the needs of teachers, students and parents. I participate in meetings, maintain a physical presence in the building and engage in activities that require my attention. I do not like to stay late at work unless I have to because doing so prevents me from being with my family as much as I desire. I make every attempt to go directly home after work. In doing this, I sacrifice going to bed early, which has been my sacrifice since I was a college student. This rhythm has worked for me for two reasons: (1) I do not have to sacrifice time with my family; and (2) I adore the night, because it allows me to think more clearly.

    I am not sure of what your role is as an educator. Perhaps you are a school leader, a teacher, staff member or district administrator but regardless, if you want to be successful in serving students then you need a rhythm that works for you. I know many successful teachers who leave work as soon as their contractual time is over in order to get home to their children whom they have not seen all day. They take work home because they choose to and are willing to do what it takes to get the job done. They are effective in their teaching and are always prepared to educate students. I also have worked with educators who spend long hours after work when students have gone home preparing for the next day, completing the work that needs to be done from their office and classroom and they do not take home any work. These educators have been successful as well and are willing to make the sacrifices necessary to complete their work. Whether you stay late or leave on time, the point is that you need to find a rhythm that works for you in order to get the job done to the best of your abilities. We all know that educating students is not an eight-hour per day job and the planning, preparation and thinking that goes into educating students requires much more time. This time that is required has a necessary rhythm that you need to find in order to live a balanced life as an educator. Sacred leaders possess a healthy state of mind and understand the importance of using time to their advantage to balance work and life. This prevents them from burning at both ends. Your rhythm, keeps you fresh, upbeat and reflective. Although burnout is a natural occurrence in education, you can delay burnout with a healthy and steady rhythm that works for you!

11

Mental Toughness

"Refuse to emotionally succumb to the negative events around you and tap your mental toughness to thrive in any environment. The good guy doesn't always win and justice doesn't always prevail, but where you direct your mental energy will always determine your attitude and it will always be controlled by you."
-Steve Siebold

Mental toughness is vital to educating students because the needs are great, the stakes are high and leadership is not for the weak hearted. The great boxer, Mike Tyson once said, "Everyone has a plan until they get hit." By the same token, my football coach used to remind us that every play drawn on the board is a touchdown, but it does not always result in a touchdown on the field. In other words, a good plan is irrelevant without great execution and a plan alone will not result in getting the job done. The reason is because, in order to successfully lead a school, you must be mentally tough and there are no shortcuts in mental toughness! For leaders, things rarely go as smoothly as planned, which is why it is crucial to have mental toughness to get through the challenges, deal with unexpected occurrences and overcome adversity and setbacks as they arise. You will experience many failures as a leader, some may be your fault while others may not. Even with the best intentions you may feel like you want give up at times, quit and think to yourself that there is no value in your efforts. However, it will require mental toughness to fight hardships and get through your darkest moments as a sacred leader. They say leadership can be a lonely place and to be honest, as a leader, I have felt that loneliness at times. If mental toughness was not a prerequisite for leadership, then more people would be successful in leading.

I do not believe that people are always born with mental toughness but I do think that it can be gained through experiences, especially from events in which leaders encounter disappointments and setbacks. Disappointments and setbacks are often what make leaders stronger and help them overcome adversity in the future if they choose to learn from failures. The challenge for a leader is that you have to be willing to embrace your failures as opportunities to learn just as much as you do your successes, if not more. Although failure is not enjoyable, if we choose to embrace our failures and learn from them, they will build our mental toughness more than our successes will.

I recall an experience I had very early in my career as a school leader of a new start up charter school. To make a long story short I was hired by an education management company out of Michigan to open a school in Columbus, Ohio, where I lived. They selected the building and location and we rushed to open the school under a very tight deadline and I had a feeling on the inside that it was not going to be successful nor would it be in the best interest of children and families, but I moved forward with the plan anyway. Ultimately, I was correct, it was a disaster but I forged on anyway giving it every ounce of effort that I had over a course of several months. To be honest, I think I had too much foolish pride to quit and hoped that things would pan out and somehow, someway it could be pulled off. I was wrong! A few months within starting the school we were only able to enroll about 100 students after getting a late start, not having supplies yet and a building that was still being renovated. I honestly could not blame parents for not sending their children to the school but that did not stop me from making every attempt to sell our educational services to families. In essence the school was budgeted for 350 students but as I stated we only had about 100, a little less to be more accurate. The bigger problem was that the management company spent money from their reserve funds to invest in getting the building ready and the expenses from construction of the facilities had drained their budget. Every time we thought we had a problem fixed a new one would arise. Who would have thought that the local fire department would require us to install a fire hydrant on the property and that alone would cost nearly $10,000.00. From the beginning the management company was bleeding in their investment in the school and after a few months, with enrollment not increasing, they wanted to recoup their funds. They had to support other schools they managed in Columbus as well as other states across the country. Since charter schools in Ohio are paid monthly from state money based upon student enrollment, there was no quick way to stop the financial hemorrhaging. The longer the school year went on, the more money investors loss. I knew that it would take time to build a quality school and I was confident in my ability to do so. I was capable of enrolling families, but time was not on my side and the management company was drowning in debt faster and faster. The only way the management company could recoup any of their investment in the facility was by making cuts to the budget which included staff reductions. One day I received a phone call from the management company's Regional Director. During the conversation he informed me that I needed to cut 33% from a three million dollar budget and I had to do it within the next 24 hours! I was forced to lay off three employees, the remaining teachers and myself took a 33% pay cut, I combined classes that they considered too small, I cut night janitorial services and ended up cleaning, vacuuming and emptying the trash in classrooms myself every night on top of being the school leader. It was one of the darkest periods of my life both personally and professional and I lost a lot of confidence, not to mention went into personal debt for years. Looking back now on that experience, it was one of the best experiences for me as a leader. Without question it was the grace of God that pulled me through. What I learned from the adversity and the process could never have been taught to me any other way and from it I grew stronger as a leader. There was no other experience that could have taught me to make such a large cut to a budget, let alone do it by myself within 24 hours. I was stretched in ways that I never thought possible and in ways I never knew I could handle. Not too many school leaders can say that they were the principal, cleaned bathrooms, mopped and vacuumed floors, emptied trash and served as the substitute teacher while receiving 33% less in their paycheck! However, I still came to work every day and did my job to the best of my abilities and served my teachers, students and parents. Students and families never knew the stress my staff and I were under. Not one of my teachers who could have quit choose to do so and I am proud to say that instruction never declined.

I would love to tell you that it had a happy ending but things got worse with the management company getting further and further in debt. Eventually, I was given one months' pay and was laid off from the job in order to save even more money. The management company decided to have the school be led by a principal from a sister school within the organization who would eventually lead the two schools to save money. They also found a contracted janitorial company to clean and made more cuts over time. In the end, I recovered by getting another job in school leadership elsewhere and the school continued to suffer financially and eventually closed its doors a couple of years later.

Words cannot express, the lesson I learned and the preparation I received during this time. The mental toughness that I developed from this experience has guided me in leadership and character development to this very day. What I learned had much more to do with character development in leadership than anything else and I am not sure that I could have learned it any other way. Mental toughness is a requirement for sacred leadership and for sacred teaching but it can only be developed and grown from experience!

12

There Will Be Conflict

"The quality of our lives depends not on whether or not we have conflicts, but on how we respond to them." -Thomas Crum

Good school leaders know that there will be conflict when leading others. There is no way of escaping conflict, but more importantly as a sacred leader, you should never run and hide from it when conflict comes your way. By intentionally avoiding conflict, you run the risk of compromising the integrity of your leadership and potentially making matters worse than they actually are. Conflict is not always extreme to the point where it has to end in bloodshed, lost lives or people disappearing and then reappearing again (remember what happened in *Avengers: End Game*). Actually, more often than not, conflict is a good thing because at a minimum it demonstrates that people are thinking, people care about what they are doing and for better or worse they are putting forth an effort to do something and make things better as they see fit.

You May Not Cause Conflict

As an administrator you may not cause the conflict or at least you may not cause it directly. This does not mean that you will not have to deal with it to some extent. By deciding to be a leader, you have chosen to face conflict whether you like it or not and whether you caused it or not. It is simply the nature of leadership and it is one of the prices you have to pay. Often times my teachers have come to me with challenges they are having and the range of these challenges vary, even extending outside of work. The challenges from work where I am leading might consist of a lack of communication, misunderstandings, disagreements about resolutions to an issue or a multitude of other reasons. If you think of a conflict, I probably have dealt with it to some degree. In my experience, issues and challenges between teachers and leaders can be resolved with little assistance and by having a conversation in which all sides are willing to listen to each other. However, there have also been occasions in which more effort has been required. When dealing with conflict between people you may want to follow these steps.

1. Listen carefully without any immediate judgment or quick response and be sure that you have heard all sides to the story. It is common for people to only tell the side that speaks to their advantage or correctness. Have the initial intent of hearing what is the root cause of the conflict.

2. Find out the expectations that people have for you. Sometimes people just want to vent, other times they may just want you to be aware of the conflict and have the intentions of solving it themselves while other times, they may want you to intervene and assist with solving the problem. You should always ask them, "How would you

like for me to help you in resolving this issue or do you want me to just listen?

3. Get all of the information that you need, although this may not mean getting all of the information that there is, because you may not have the time to do so depending on the urgency of the conflict. After you feel that you have the information that you need and have talked to the parties involved, get those individuals who the conflict involves in the same room. I warn you to be selective because some people may not have healthy intentions in resolving the issue. Under no circumstance do you want to create a sideshow. People gravitate towards negative drama and it can also be a distraction to solving the real issue.

4. Lastly, start working on a resolution and consider all options. When considering the options, think about who the conflict is

impacting, the urgency of the matter, the time that is needed to implement a resolution and doing what is fair. This does not mean, that everyone will be happy because in conflict all sides are rarely pleased with the outcome. The intent is not to make everyone happy. The intent is to resolve the issue with fairness and ensure that the success of the school continues to occur.

Do Not Run

Your reputation and effectiveness as a leader can be predicated on how you deal with conflict. Teachers and staff members watch what administrators do but more importantly they observe what school leaders do not do. If you do not confront conflict, or worse, run from it, you will lose the respect of your teachers and staff, and even worst than that, you will hurt your reputation as a school leader. Sacred leaders serve teachers and students. Administrators cannot serve others if they are running away. Not to mention, you could be running to a much bigger problem or creating another one if you choose to run.

Conflict is rarely easy but in a lot of cases it will make you stronger if you do not run. Running makes you tired and weak so do not do it! I have seen administrators try to avoid conflict by not addressing it, ignoring the problem and abandoning their teachers to solve the conflict on their own when they needed help from the school leader because they were not in a position to resolve the conflict. This created a larger problem, things got worse and respect was lost for the principal. Never forget that sacred leaders deal with conflict head on and know that in doing so, they are also doing their job.

Conflicts Come and Go Like Storms

Conflicts are a lot like storms. They come and they go but they never last forever. Also, like storms, conflicts were not created for us to get over, they are meant for us to get through. Sometimes you need to be brave and face what you are experiencing, deal with the consequences of bad decisions and confront your enemies directly. No one can physically get over a storm, literally speaking, because they are too big. So you must prepare to get through it.

When putting storms in a literal context, we know that occasionally some storms are unexpected, but rarely so. Real storms typically have signs that they are coming our way. These signs include; a drop in temperature, large billowy clouds, dark clouds, dimming of the sky and sometimes lightning. A sacred leader who is in tuned with their school environment, will often see the signs of conflict in their school environment as it is coming. When these signs are happening be sure to pay close attention and do not take these signs lightly so that you can be as prepared as possible. Knowing what issues may cause potential conflict in your school can only be done if you have an intuition about your teachers, students, parents, community and school environment. The best way to be prepared is to stay prepared in what you are doing as a sacred leader. No one can know every storm that will come, as some storms are unexpected. However, I still think that there are signs if administrators pay attention and develop their intuition. This will help them see more storms coming, than not.

Keep the mindset that conflict can and will arise at some point but do not be a paranoid leader. Just hold on to the fact that conflict will arise, invited or uninvited, directly related to you and indirectly related to you. When storms come in the form of conflicts, sacred leaders work with others to arrive at the best resolution to solve them.

13

Stay Calm

"Calmness is a human superpower. The ability to not overreact to not take things personally keeps your mind clear and your heart at peace."
-Marcandangel

I firmly believe that the overall attitudes of the adults and culture of a school building reflect the leadership in the building. I also firmly believe that the attitudes of students and culture of a classroom reflect the teacher who is educating students in that classroom. Yes, I do think that there are some exceptions and some outliers that exist, but for the most part, in my experience, these beliefs hold true. This is why I wanted to write a chapter on the importance of staying calm. The catch is, calmness does not come from the outside, calmness is an inner energy and belief that is projected outwardly from a person who is feeling it inwardly. Calmness is your ability to control how you respond to circumstances and situations that may not be in your favor. It does not mean that on the inside you do not feel anxiety, worry, stress, anger or frustration because these are all natural emotions. Your calmness is a result of being able to control your emotions and responses to situations and circumstances that hinder your production and service to others. It is also an inward feeling that lets you know that, no matter how difficult the conflict or challenge may be, everything will work out in the end. Sacred leaders and sacred educators alike, face challenges that are unexpected and these challenges reveal our character to ourselves as well as others. They show others our ability to handle unexpected circumstances and stressful situations. They also divulge our emotional maturity.

From a leadership standpoint, it has always been clear to me that few people would ever follow a leader who lacks control over their emotions or responds to situations like "the sky is falling." No matter how bad things are, the sky will never fall! In reality there are some good days and some bad days but most days fall somewhere in between. <u>The Road Less Traveled</u> by Scott Peck, MD, records two of my favorite quotes. One states, "Life is nothing but a series of problems." The other declares, "Life is difficult, but once you accept that life is difficult it no longer becomes difficult."

In order to remain calm in situations where you want to actually lose your mind, you need to accept the fact that bad things will occur, understand that all situations will not go your way and acknowledge the reality that you will be disappointed by people. These are simply a way a life and are some of the things that make life difficult for educators. If you choose to serve as a sacred leader, it means you also accept the challenges that come with it. Great challenges produce great strength. Each challenge that you overcome with a calm, patient and faithful demeanor builds your confidence that things will work out as they should.

Emotions are a part of life and you cannot always control how you feel, but you can control how you react to how you are feeling. As a sacred leader, staying calm during intense situations will matriculate down to teachers and staff members and eventually will reflect in the attitudes and behaviors of students. Show me a school building where students are out of control, unruly, tense and noncompliant, and I will show you the same things about the adults in the building.

Staying calm may appear as being weak or uncaring but in actuality it takes strength, discipline and maturity. Anyone can flip out like a toddler but it requires a mature leader to control his or her emotions in situations and circumstances where they want to lose their cool or have a temper tantrum. Staying calm requires a level of confidence in knowing that things are not perfect and that is okay. Having calmness sends the message to people around you that you believe in them, the work that they do and you are willing to help them work through any and all difficulties. When you possess the ability to stay calm it will change your school culture for the better. It demonstrates that no challenge is too great for the team to overcome.

14

Know the Landscape

"Be a yardstick of quality. Some people aren't used to an environment where excellence is expected."
-Steve Jobs

The word landscape when used as a verb means, *"to make more attractive by altering the existing design, adding ornamental features, and planting trees and shrubs."* As a leader you are probably not changing trees and shrubs (or maybe you are) in the literal sense. However, your focus should be changing the environment, based on how it looks, how it feels, how it sounds and the message it sends. This will enable people to ultimately work to change themselves. It is important to remember that changing the landscape and not the people is most essential. Individuals change themselves if they choose to change. Changing people often requires too much time and effort which is something you do not always have at your disposal, as a leader. You have a purpose, a mission and people to serve. When individuals are stuck on fighting you because you want to make them better and they are resistant to improving, you can lose valuable time fighting them back. You have to be selective in where you direct your energy and know that not everyone wants to improve. Some people are stuck in meeting the minimum standard. Still others even function below the minimum. I urge you not to spend your time on people who are not focused on improving.

The landscape is what you see and what you feel as it relates to the school environment. You can take two similar homes with different landscapes and one may feel welcoming and appealing while a another one looks dilapidated and repulsive. A great landscape can make an average looking home appear captivating and alluring which improves the overall appeal of the home. As a principal, I view my school in a similar light. I believe in working to ensure that the front office is a friendly, clean and inviting place that reflects high standards, an excellence for learning and a love for children. My belief is that the front office sets the tone for the school being perceived as a place of high achievement. Therefore, the front office should be free of disruptive behaviors, chaos and loud noises. No matter what school I have led, I have never wanted students who are misbehaving to be in the front office just sitting. When someone enters the office I do not want students who are guilty of misconduct to serve as a representation of the rest of the student body, the teachers or the learning that is occurring. I want the representation of students and the environment of the school to reflect positivity and productivity in education.

As a sacred leader, knowing the landscape requires you to be detail-oriented. You must also possess the empathy needed to put yourself in another's shoes. Ask yourself, how people feel when they enter the doors of your building. Do they feel that your school is one that reflects love, is nurturing and caring? Are students engaged in activities that help to develop their minds, or is it a place that is uninviting, that represents confusion, disengagement and a detriment to the lives of children and their learning. As a leader you are responsible for how people feel when they enter your building, how students feel when they are at school and how teachers feel about the support they need to be successful in teaching students. Know you school's landscape and if it is not one that is of the highest quality, then it is imperative that you work to improve it as a sacred leader.

15

Love and Gratitude

"When we focus on our gratitude, the tide of disappointment goes out, and the tide of love rushes in."
-Kristin Armstrong

Trust me when I tell you, nothing goes as far in leadership as leading with love and gratitude for the opportunity you have to serve others. Love and gratitude can take you places that a degree and experience can never take you. Everyone wants to feel appreciated and loved and as a school leader you have the ability to demonstrate love and gratitude to people on a daily basis and honestly, that should be your ultimate goal. Knowing that this is the case, I often wonder why love and gratitude is missing from so many schools. I believe that in order to move forward and get more accomplished, leaders need to first learn the essence of leading with love and demonstrating gratitude for the people around them. Teachers come to work and they receive a paycheck. Students come to school to receive an education. However, both teachers and students want to work and learn in a school environment where they feel there is love and gratitude. Do not get me wrong, a paycheck is nice and getting an education is important but the icing on the cake is the demonstration of love and gratitude for human beings. I want to feel that everyone feels loved and everyone feels appreciated but that is simply not the case. I was once talking to all of my 4th grade students during a small assembly when I asked, "Who has been told, *I love you today?*" and only about 15-20 hands went up in the air out of approximately 140 students. I was shocked and confounded because personally I feel that everyone, especially children, should hear someone tell them, *"I love you,"* every day. Thinking back on the experience I wish I had asked the teachers in the room the same question because teachers also need to be told that they are loved and appreciated daily as well. If your aim is to be an effective school administrator then start with love and gratitude. Consider what ways you can spread love and demonstrate gratitude in your school. Think about ways you can show that you appreciate people for being at school. Never assume that receiving a paycheck or receiving a good education is enough. Sacred leaders always extend love and show gratitude to those they are responsible for leading.

16

None Of Your Business

"You can't change how people treat you or what they say about you. All you can do is change how you react to it." -Unknown

You may not like everyone and in reality not everyone will like you. Some people will not like your decisions even if those decisions are in their best interest. Others may not like you because of the mistakes you have made. Hopefully, you have not personally offended anyone. If so, apologize, do not do it again and move on. In other situations, there will be people who do not care much for your personality based upon what they experience with you. In a nutshell, there are millions of reasons why people may not like you and the reasons may or may not be legitimate. When you are a school leader, if you are doing the best that you can do, you are growing, becoming better and your aim is to take care of students, teachers and your staff, then keep moving forward. There is no way possible to please everyone all of the time. In fact, by trying to do so, you can experience a host of failure!

One of the reasons that people will not like you is because they do not understand you or your position. In fact, as a school leader most people only get to see you professionally and never as husband, wife, father, mother, brother, sister, uncle, aunt or otherwise. They may not believe that you have a sense of humor, have family issues or health concerns. They may not believe you deal with "real" issues outside of work. This is not terrible, but as a sacred leader you need to understand that their perspective of you is primarily based upon their interactions with you at work. Therefore, any negative judgment is limited in it's foundation.

Not being liked by everyone is part of sacred leadership and goes with the territory. The leader that everyone likes is probably trying to be everything to everyone but stands for nothing. The moment you begin to stand for something that is against what other people represent, even when it is in the best interest of students, it will cause controversy. Have you ever known an effective leader who was not considered controversial at some point? That is part of leadership. If you are constantly going with the flow, trying to always make people happy then you might just be a manager at best, maintaining the status quo. People will always have their opinions of what you should do, where you need to be, what you ought to say or even how you should think. Maybe they are right, but maybe not. I think that if someone knows how you should be as a leader better than you do, they should consider becoming the leader.

I am an avid sports fan and I feel I have the right to have my personal opinion about the performance of my favorite athletes and teams. As a true fan I keep in mind three things One, the athletes I am criticizing are much better athletes than I will ever be or have ever been. Secondly, I only see their performance during the game and I do not know enough about them personally to form a true opinion about who they are or their character (in most cases). So, I tend to limit my criticism. I only critique their athletic performance. I have always wondered why so many athletes get emotional and respond to the criticism they receive from fans, especially when the fans who are giving the criticism are either spending an exorbitant amount of time and money watching them. It should not be the athlete's desire to know what fans think about their performance. Fans, do not have enough insight on who the athlete is as a person, or the work that they have done to get to where they are. The only opinions athletes should be concerned with are coaches and teammates. Leaders often get too caught up in what everyone thinks about them and when they do they lose their focus. What other people think of you is not your business, what you think of yourself is.

17

Embrace Your Experiences

"The only source of knowledge is our experience."
-Albert Einstein

I remember earning my undergraduate degree and feeling so proud, but also feeling that I was not any smarter than I was the day before simply because I earned a degree. Then, several years later I earned my master's degree and I thought, this was it, surely I increased my intelligence to the level of a superhero, imagining I would become the next Tony Starks (aka Iron Man) but again, I did not feel any more intelligent nor did I feel wiser during the days prior to earning my master's degree. I am in no way implying that earning a college degree is not important nor do I want to downplay the values of a college degree. To be honest, earning my degree has opened many doors and has provided me with the opportunity to provide for my family. Over time, I have learned that our experiences increase our wisdom as leaders more so than any degree. It is true that experience is the best teacher and that includes both good and bad experiences as well as the experiences of others. There is no degree on earth that is offered that can prepare you for life better than the experiences that life provides you with. The most important thing about your experiences as a sacred leader is that they are ultimately preparing you to do your job better as time goes along and that is more valuable than a college degree.

Have you ever worked with someone who is fresh out of college or just obtained a graduate degree, but has little or no life experience? They typically (not in all cases) are so excited by their well-earned success and book knowledge that they have little clue that experience is also a prerequisite for success and experience only comes with time. I am an avid reader and my collection of books is large. However, as a leader I still understand that even my books have limitations and I cannot lead from the pages of books. It is my experiences that matter most. At some point you have to put down the books or whatever you are reading and experience life. In sacred leadership the only thing you will have that will help you and support you, at times, will be your experiences. This happens because not every book was written with you in mind (except this one...lol). Your experiences in various areas of life will often serve as your greatest mentors. Those experiences will come from how you were raised in childhood, your relationships with people, your successes and most importantly your failures. Both good and bad experiences need to be embraced. Keeping them in your mind makes them readily available for the point at which you need them again.

I have come to understand that in leadership your childhood may play a greater influence than you realize or are willing to accept. Your experiences with personal and professional relationships, experiences with family and experiences with friends will influence your leadership. Never underestimate your past experiences, devalue, downplay or overlook events from your childhood, relationships and previous personal or professional experiences because they will serve you tremendously in your role as a sacred leader.

18

Protect Your Ears

"Don't entertain negative energy. Some situations will test your patience and try to make you overreact, overthink, and respond to things that don't deserve your life force. Your attention is your power. Don't feed what doesn't add value to your life. Protect your energy."
-averstu.com

There is an old saying, "garbage in, garbage out," and I believe it means if you hear and listen to garbage then that is what will consume your thoughts and come out of your mouth either intentionally or unintentionally. The same can be said for the influence of listening to people who talk negatively. If negativity, doubts and fears are the constant topics of conversations that you listen to, then that is what will consume your mind and eventually be the content of the words you speak. I urge you as a sacred leader to be careful of what and who you listen to. Have you ever been feeling good, having an awesome day, appreciating life, thankful to God, valuing your loved ones, and feeling blessed for good health? Then, out of nowhere, you find yourself listening to people who have different circumstances than you. They are ungrateful and before you know it, you wind up devaluing your wonderful life just by listening to their negative words. This occurs because your thoughts are impacted by what you listen to on television, what you read on social media and the conversations that you hear from those around you. I cannot stress enough the importance of protecting your ears as a leader and refusing to be negatively impacted by others.

As I have grown as a leader, I am much more interested in the energy of others than I am the content of their conversations. If you are not careful, you may unconsciously adopt negative thinking and beliefs that are not even your own. This may lead you to become negative and embrace a negative mindset. It is imperative that you protect your own thoughts and beliefs and this is difficult to do if you are consumed with listening to negative conversations from others. As a sacred leader, you are leading other people and because of your purpose, it is imperative that you are even more aware of who you spend your time listening to. Guard your mind against negativity, doubt and fear. Do not simply accept the thinking of others before you dissect it for yourself and determine whether it is the truth or a lie. As a sacred leader, you need to be very conscious of the conversations that enter your mind so that you do not hinder your growth, development or downplay the wonderful possibilities of leadership that you possess. Under no circumstance should you simply accept negative thinking or talking as truth because it will have a damaging impact on your leadership.

SACRED CULTURE

19

Adapting to Change

"It is not the strongest of the species that survives; nor the most intelligent that survives. It is the one that is most adaptable to change."
-Charles Darwin

You cannot change everything and sometimes good things fall apart. All educational systems have their flaws while some educational systems are completely broken. It needs to be understood that no educational system is completely perfect but that is okay, because it is not the system that makes the difference, it is the people in the system that make the difference. School culture is an ongoing effort that is never without needed improvements. The mistake that I often see with creating a healthy school culture is, when educators make the assumption that changing school culture is a quick fix process that occurs in a few days, weeks or months. In actuality, in order to change school culture there has to be an ongoing process that can take months or even years. Currently in the field of education, we have an influx of Edu-Heroes that use social media to share their stories of success in improving school culture. These Edu-Heroes and their stories are placed in the public eye and tales of the hard work that they have done and what they have accomplished in school improvement influences many people. They are even placed on pedestals by other educators who admire their work or want to learn the secrets of their success in order to duplicate it at their own schools with the aim of improving school culture and climate. However, the reality is, heroes who accomplish anything worthy of doing, never do it by themselves. To effectively change school culture it first requires strong leadership. But, even with strong leadership, that is not enough because it will also require a strong group of teachers and support staff in the process. I once read, *"Leaders don't change people, they create environments where people change themselves."* This quote speaks to the crucial element of understanding the process for improving school culture and what is most essential. When you focus only on the adults and students you can easily become unfocused, distracted and lose your way. Yet, when you focus on the environment and the needs of the environment, change then becomes more likely to occur with adults and children. In some instances the needs of the environment require that more support is given to teachers by administrators. It may also mean that there needs to be clarity of expectations and an understanding of what occurs when those expectations are not fully met. The environment may require calmness, peace and cultivation in order for it to be welcoming and inviting to others. Whatever the environment needs is what the team must be willing to provide and that, in itself, closes the gap on a potentially broken system.

Changing people can be exhausting and requires time that you may not have. The needs are great when it comes to people, so it is always wiser to narrow the focus but do so with intensity to make the change that you want to happen. The environment can be changed and influenced with less stress and anxiety. It can have a much greater impact for those within the school environment as well. You cannot change people, but you can influence people to change themselves and that alone has a great impact on the sacred culture of the school.

20

Fresh Starts

"You may have a fresh start any moment you choose, for this thing we call 'failure' is not the falling down, but the staying down."
-Mary Pickford

Changing behaviors has a lot to do with fresh starts and it does not always mean waiting for a new day but instead may require starting over in the moment. Sometimes fresh starts need to be within minutes of each other. I like to encourage my teachers to build healthy relationships, communicate with parents, employ incentives, administer consequences and allow students to reflect on their behavior. One of the ways my teachers respond to misbehaviors is by allowing students to take a timeout within the classroom. Some students may choose to do this on their own if they are having a difficult time with self-regulating. The timeout space is a location in the classroom where students can go to reflect on their actions and attitude by thinking or writing for a brief period time. This space is within view of the teacher and rest of the class so a student can still see and hear everything that is going on. Students are not permitted to be there for long durations of time. So typically a timeout it lasts about five to ten minutes, depending upon the age of the student. Once they return to the rest of the class they receive what is most important about timeout, a fresh start to demonstrate that they can correct their behavior or attitude by doing things differently. What I do not want from teachers after a timeout is ridicule, a grudge held against students, resentment or missed opportunities to start over. Timeouts also afford the teacher an opportunity to provide a fresh start. I like to think of fresh starts as a way of demonstrating forgiveness for what was done incorrectly and as an opportunity for students to change. Even as adults we need forgiveness, time to reflect on our behaviors and opportunities to change them for the better. You have to be willing to practice forgiveness and give fresh starts within the day, in the moment and not only from day to day. The greatest teachers that I have ever worked with have been the most effective in the lives of children because they possessed two qualities that matter most, LOVE and FORGIVENESS. Both are things that our children need desperately, especially if school is the only place in their lives where they receive them. Fresh starts are very much associated with LOVE and FORGIVENESS and both are essential to a sacred school culture.

21

Don't Throw Stones

"You will never reach your destination if you stop and throw stones at every dog that barks."
-Winston Churchill

If you want to improve school culture then you have to avoid throwing stones. The phrase throwing stones does not literally mean, throwing stones, rocks or pebbles. It is a phrase used to warn against judging or commenting on how others live their lives. It can also mean not blaming or pointing the finger at others before examining yourself. Things will happen that you do not want to happen and you will make mistakes right along with everyone else. To improve school culture, you have to meet people where they are and have the understanding that not everyone will see things as you do. This can be frustrating but it can also provide opportunities for you to learn about new things or develop different ways of handling challenges all while learning more about people.

School culture is often destroyed when the adults are throwing stones or blaming one another for failures or setbacks. Everyone has faults and shortcomings and school culture is no different. This is because a sacred school culture is not made up on the beliefs and values of one person, it requires a collective effort from everyone! The essential thing is for people to be willing to work together for the greater good of doing whatever is right, and in the best interest of children and families. Doing right by students should be where you place your primary focus and attention. A sacred school culture is embedded with focus on building off of the strengths of others, not throwing stones. Chances are, if you are throwing stones, you probably have several stones being thrown back at you.

If you want people to forgive you for your mistakes, then you might want to extend forgiveness to others for their indiscretions. Choosing not to throw stones is about forgiveness, understanding, acceptance and most importantly, working together to change school culture. If you are a school leader, then this quality will be appreciated by those you are leading. If you are a teacher, then your students will value your forgiveness and grow in ways that extend beyond academics. When you choose to throw stones, it is likely that you may eventually run out of stones and find that the problem falls back to you. On the other hand, if you choose to forgive, then forgiveness will be given back to you for your wrongdoing, because we all have made mistakes, have shortcomings and are not void of error. Do not throw stones. Instead, choose to forgive. Practice letting go of wrong doing, accept that we all have flaws and are in need of people who will help us grow.

22

The Kind of School You Want

"Remember, the change you want to see in the world, and in your school begins with you."
-Joseph Clementi

Would you send your own children to your school? Even if you do not have children, if you did, would you send them to your school? I have asked myself this question every year since being a principal and I have always been able to say, "yes" even if at times it has come later in the year or in my second year at the school. I also ask myself when I am hiring a teacher, would I put my children, whom I love dearly, in this person's class? If the answer is "no," then I do not offer them the job unless I do not have any other options (I have been in that position before as well). The point of the question to is to reflect on how well you believe in your school culture. Are the standards that you have for your school and classroom culture high enough or do you have the attitude that the students you are responsible for educating are other people's children so they do not get your very best every day? In order to cultivate a sacred school culture you must have high expectations, not only for students but for yourself. Perhaps your answer is "no" because of how students behave. If so, work to change the behaviors. Maybe, it is "no" due to the quality of teaching. If so, you can improve that as well. The best way to evaluate your school culture is to decide if the school you are in is the school that you would want for your own children.

23

Identity Crisis

"The identity crisis...occurs in that period of the life cycle when each youth must forge himself some central perspective and direction, some working unity, out of the effective remnants of his childhood and the hopes of his anticipated adulthood."
-Erik Erikson

When students are of school age they are still learning a lot about the world around them, about people and perhaps most importantly, themselves. During this same time, it is not unlikely that students will experience an identity crisis. Students want the approval of their parents and caregivers prior to coming to school. Then they begin school and the approval of parents or caregivers may become secondary because now they have been introduced to their peers. They want healthy interactions with their classmates and begin to develop friendships with other students they attend school with. They actively seek validation and approval from people in their age range and want to receive confirmation that they are liked and accepted. Over a period of time, the identity crisis can worsen, especially when students do not have a solid foundation as to who they are and when they do not have support at home. As children grow and continue in their schooling they also grow into adolescents and peer interaction become even more important. Over time, friendships are made and when the influences of social media are thrown into the mix, youth begin to make comparisons between themselves and those around them. With the influences of social media, the struggle for youth to avoid having an identity crisis becomes even more difficult.

The challenge that educators face, is getting to know and understand who their students really are and not just who students project themselves to be at school. This can be particularly complex when students project themselves in ways that do not reflect who they really are and it results in them being labeled *thug, troublemaker, lazy* or *crazy* and the list goes on.

There are students who might quietly be suffering from an identity crisis. These students can have a low self-esteem, suffer from depression and have a feeling of loneliness. However, educators can mistakenly perceive them as good students because they abide by rules, they are compliant and do not cause trouble. These same students could actually be ticking time bombs ready to do something that will endanger the lives of their peers and adults. Perhaps there are also some students who display negative behaviors because it is a defense mechanism used to prevent people from getting too close to them. I have witnessed students behave in disruptive ways and pretend to be tough as a survival skill to endure living in their communities. It is not that these students always wanted to carry a hard exterior, but they used it as a defense mechanism to protect themselves from outside forces. It was not a true reflection of their identity nor the identity they projected at school.

It is hard as an educator not to get upset and become angry at some at the behaviors and actions of students, especially when they can be disruptive to teaching and learning. I do not want to excuse disruptive behaviors and imply that any ongoing disruptive behaviors should not have their set of consequences. However, I do want to say that there are sometimes deeper reasons for the disruptive behaviors and those reasons may be the result of an identity crisis that students could be going through.

It is not uncommon for students to have multiple identities that they switch between from home to school and among friends. I have had students who were viewed as disrespectful and argumentative. As a result, their responses to their teacher's instructions and redirection were not positive. As teachers have gotten to know these same students over time, they realized that those students were suffering from an identity crisis because when they had adult responsibilities at home they were being treated like adults by their parents. Then, when they arrived at school where the expectation is for them to behave like students their age, there was a conflict. Their identity may have been appropriate at home because they were being treated like an adult. However, at school the teachers needed them to be students who acted their age. This shift between home and school impacts a lot of students with adult responsibilities outside of school. Identity crises are very common in children, adolescents and youth. The adults responsible for their education have to be sensitive to the their identity crisis and acknowledge that this could very well be the root of the problem they are experiencing in their lives.

Do not rush to judge students, especially based on outer appearances or based on your own personal biases. Never take for granted that you know all that there is to know as a result of the behaviors that you see. It is not uncommon for students who are experiencing an identity crisis to lack an understanding of their great potential, and you might be the key that helps them to unlock it. This can be done by meeting your students where they are and focusing on their potential. The potential of a student's greatness as seen by you is what may help them achieve wonders within the sacred school community and in life.

24

The Trend of Trauma

"Avoid the crowd. Do your own thinking independently. Be the chess player and not the chess piece."
-Ralph Charell

Education tends to adopt trends, topics and certain "hot" words that spread through education with much popularity. It only takes a nice catch phrase, acronym or "cool" words and BOOM, the trend is set and it is quickly devoured in the minds of educators around the world. Not to mention, let it catch on for a few months and everyone you know becomes an "expert" on whatever the new trend is. The trends become the subject of professional development, money-making opportunities, hot topics for writing books and you will be bombarded with emails from people or organizations that can help you become better at whatever is trending. I am not against trends, innovation or even new found discoveries that truly improve education because education for students and teachers needs to be in constant evolution and improvement. I am against the trends that educators jump on without thinking or deciding whether or not they meet their needs or the needs of their students. I am also against overusing trends for the sake of just doing something, while not processing the effectiveness or need.

As sacred educators we need to carefully consider the needs of our students and not be lazy thinkers by applying trends that do not relate to our situations simply because they become popular. It is not right to use trends as a crutch to over-label students, over-analyze them and ignore the real issues. The acceptance of trends without thinking carefully creates surface level solutions to the deeper issues at hand that require more work. Trends should not be utilized to develop an obsession for categorizing students when educators need to have a clear understanding of a child's development, influences from parental involvement, community norms or simply a lack of adult supervision.

Trauma is defined as a, *"deeply distressing or disturbing experience"*. For many, this can be a broad definition. The circumstances determine the severity of the trauma. I do believe in trauma and I know after working in education for over 20 years that trauma is very real. I have seen it daily in the lives of some of the children and families that I have served. My students have been impacted directly by physical, sexual and mental abuse. They have lived through neglect, death of parents and a host of other factors. I have had many students clinically diagnosed with mental health issues such as high anxiety, depression, Bipolar, ADD, ADHD and ODD as well as other mental health challenges. So, I truly think that trauma is something that educators face daily. The argument of whether or not trauma is real is not the point I am trying to make. I would like educators to examine whether or not we, as professionals, are appropriately identifying students as having trauma. Could it be that we part of some "group thinking" in which a lot of children are labeled as having trauma when, in fact, they may just be facing the challenges that life provides? I want us to consider whether or not we are haphazardly labeling children as having trauma when they may be experiencing common or uncommon issues of childhood. There are instances in life when students have to learn to persevere, develop their grit and learn not to give up. Students need to learn that life is unfair but with hard work, love, support, and, focus they can achieve their dreams. These are just great life skills for all students whether they have experienced trauma or not. I am not here to tell you what is or what is not trauma in the lives of your students, that is not for me to determine. I do want to encourage you not to jump on the bandwagon and assume that if a child does not have a perfect home life, or their parents' values do not match your own and if they are displaying behaviors that you do not understand that they are somehow traumatized students.

Conclusion

I am deeply grateful for my years in education. I honestly believe I have the second best job in the world as a school principal (number one would be owning an NFL team). I have the opportunity every day to positively impact the lives of people. That does not mean that the work is anywhere near easy or that there are days when I do not want to go to work because that is a reality with any job, in my opinion. However, I know that God has called me to this sacred profession and I am committed to serving in education in some capacity for as long as I am able to do so. There are millions of educators around the world who feel as I do and maybe a few who do not. Regardless, I want you to know that I appreciate the work that you do, your service to students and their families and the sacrifices that you make. Educating students, regardless of where you serve is not for the weak hearted, not for quitters and definitely not for those who are incapable of demonstrating love and patience to students. I simply want to tell you, thank you for all that you have done, all that you do and all that you will do. I appreciate you dearly. I hope that this book has served as some inspiration to continue on in your sacred service to the lives of our future generations. Never Give Up!

Notes
Soul of Teaching

The Divine & Splendid

Allure of Being Busy

The Right Swing

Limitations

Never Lose Your Humanity

Stay Focused

Being Nice

It's About Will Power

Late Night Rhythms

Mental Toughness

There Will Be Conflict

Stay Calm

Know the Landscape

Love and Gratitude

None of Your Business

Embrace Your Experience

Protect Your Ears

Adapting to Change

Fresh Starts

Don't Throw Stones

The Kind of Schools You Want

Identity Crisis

The Trend of Trauma

A Sacred Place For Learning: *Teaching, Leading & Culture*

Additional Notes

About the Author

Mr. Naim Sanders has served children and families in the field of education for 20 years as a teacher, principal, charter school developer and leader. He has worked as an educational consultant with the Ohio Department of Education, adjunct professor for Notre Dame College and faculty supervisor for Grand Canyon University. Mr. Sanders is the author of several books including: *The Beautiful Struggles of Coming of Age*, *The Beautiful Struggles off Teaching*, *The Beautiful Struggles of Teaching Workbook* and *A Sacred Place For Learning: Teaching, Leading & Culture*.

For comments, questions or to engage in further dialogue about what you have read please contact the author!

The Beautiful Struggles of Coming of Age
The Beautiful Struggles of Teaching
The Beautiful Struggles of Teaching Workbook

Contact Information

www.naimsanders.com

naimanders@gmail.com

Naimauthorpage

@NaimSanders

naimsanders

Made in the USA
Monee, IL
12 January 2021